W9-AAT-801

Accordion to Zeppelin

Inventions from A to Z

Mary Elizabeth Salzmann

Consulting Editor, Diane Craig, M.A./Reading Specialist

ABDO
Publishing Company

Published by ABDO Publishing Company, 8000 West 78th Street, Edina, Minnesota 55439. Copyright © 2009 by Abdo Consulting Group, Inc. International copyrights reserved in all countries. No part of this book may be reproduced in any form without written permission from the publisher. Super SandCastle™ is a trademark and logo of ABDO Publishing Company.

Printed in the United States.

Editor: Pam Price
Content Developer: Nancy Tuminelly
Cover and Interior Design and Production: Colleen Dolphin, Mighty Media
Photo Credits: iStockphoto/calvio, iStockphoto/Oktay Ortakcioglu, iStockphoto/Eliza Snow, iStockphoto/Steven van Soldt, iStockphoto/Luis Carlos Torres, Photodisc, ShutterStock, Stockbyte

Library of Congress Cataloging-in-Publication Data

Salzmann, Mary Elizabeth, 1968-

   Accordion to Zeppelin : inventions from A to Z / Mary Elizabeth Salzmann.

   p. cm. -- (Let's look A to Z)

   ISBN 978-1-60453-008-7

   1. Inventions--Miscellanea--Juvenile literature. I. Title.

   T48.S35 2008

   600--dc22

                     2007050952

Super SandCastle™ books are created by a team of professional educators, reading specialists, and content developers around five essential components—phonemic awareness, phonics, vocabulary, text comprehension, and fluency—to assist young readers as they develop reading skills and strategies and increase their general knowledge. All books are written, reviewed, and leveled for guided reading, early reading intervention, and Accelerated Reader® programs for use in shared, guided, and independent reading and writing activities to support a balanced approach to literacy instruction.

Publishing Company

About Super SandCastle™

Bigger Books for Emerging Readers
Grades K–4

Created for library, classroom, and at-home use, Super SandCastle™ books support and engage young readers as they develop and build literacy skills and will increase their general knowledge about the world around them. Super SandCastle™ books are part of SandCastle™, the leading preK–3 imprint for emerging and beginning readers. Super SandCastle™ features a larger trim size for more reading fun.

Let Us Know

Super SandCastle™ would like to hear your stories about reading this book. What was your favorite page? Was there something hard that you needed help with? Share the ups and downs of learning to read. We want to hear from you! Send us an e-mail.

sandcastle@abdopublishing.com

Contact us for a complete list of SandCastle™, Super SandCastle™, and other nonfiction and fiction titles from ABDO Publishing Company.

www.abdopublishing.com • 8000 West 78th Street Edina, MN 55439 • 800-800-1312 • 952-831-1632 fax

This fun and informative series employs illustrated definitions to introduce emerging readers to an alphabet of words in various topic areas. Each page combines words with corresponding images and descriptive sentences to encourage learning and knowledge retention. AlphagalorZ inspires young readers to find out more about the subjects that most interest them!

The "Guess what?" feature expands the reading and learning experience by offering additional information and fascinating facts about specific words or concepts. The "More Words" section provides additional related A to Z vocabulary words that develop and increase reading comprehension.

These books are appropriate for library, classroom, and home use.

Aa

Accordion

An accordion is a musical instrument with a keyboard and a bellows.

The bellows is used to push air through the accordion. Pressing the keys changes the notes.

The accordion was patented in Austria by Cyrill Demian in 1829.

Balloon

English scientist Michael Faraday invented the rubber balloon in 1824. He used balloons in experiments with hydrogen. Most modern balloons are made of latex.

Guess what?

Before the rubber balloon, people made balloons out of animal bladders and intestines.

Bb

Can Opener

The first can opener was
patented in 1858 by Ezra
Warner. It looked like
a small curved saw with
a pointed end. It was used
mostly by the military
during the Civil War.

Cc

Guess what?

Before paper straws were invented, people used hollow grasses, such as straw, to drink through. That's why they were called straws.

Drinking Straw

In 1888, Marvin Stone invented a way to make drinking straws by winding strips of paper around a small rod. The straws were coated with wax so they wouldn't get soggy when people used them.

Eyeglasses

Eyeglasses were invented in Italy around 1280. No one knows who was the first to make them. The first eyeglasses didn't have arms. You had to balance them on your nose or hold them with your hand.

Ee

Guess what?

Eyeglasses with arms weren't invented until nearly 1700.

Ferris Wheel

Guess what?

Music for the first Ferris wheel was provided by a live band that rode in one of the cars.

The Ferris wheel was invented by George W. Ferris. He designed it for the Chicago World's Fair in 1893. This first Ferris wheel was 264 feet tall. It had 36 cars, and each car could carry 60 people.

Ff

Gum

People have chewed tree sap and resin for thousands of years. In 1848, John B. Curtis became the first person to make and sell chewing gum as a product. It was called State of Maine Pure Spruce Gum.

Gg

Guess what?

The first bubble gum was called Blibber-Blubber.

Hh

Guess what?

Some historians believe Thomas Jefferson invented the wooden coat hanger.

Hanger

The wire coat hanger was invented by Albert J. Parkhouse in 1903. Elmer D. Rogers designed the hanger with a cardboard bar in 1935.

Ice Hockey

Ice hockey grew out of various field games in which players hit balls with curved sticks. In places with cold winters, people would play these games on frozen lakes and rivers. The first organized game that was most like modern ice hockey was played in Montreal, Canada, in 1875.

Jigsaw Puzzle

The first jigsaw puzzle was made by John Spilsbury in 1766. He was an English mapmaker, and his jigsaw puzzles had pictures of maps. Early jigsaw puzzles were made of wood. Now most of them are made of cardboard.

Guess what?

A jigsaw puzzle called "Life: The Great Challenge" has 24,000 pieces. It is about 5 feet wide and 14 feet long.

Kk

Guess what?

Dean Gitter converted a grain silo into a giant kaleidoscope. It is in Catskill Corners, New York.

Kaleidoscope

Scottish scientist Sir David Brewster invented the kaleidoscope in 1816. A kaleidoscope is a tube with mirrors at one end. The tube is filled with colored glass or plastic. When you look through the tube while rotating it, you see changing color patterns.

Lawn Mower

The lawn mower was invented in 1830 by English engineer Edwin Beard Budding. It was a reel mower similar to the ones some people still use today. The first motorized lawn mower was invented by James Sumner in 1893.

Matchbook

The matchbook was invented in 1889 by Pennsylvania lawyer Joshua Pusey. At the time, matches were made of wood and came in boxes that were too big to fit in a pocket. Pusey thought that matches made of paper strips bound together would be easier to carry around.

Mm

Neon Sign

When electricity is applied to a glass bulb filled with neon gas, it creates an orange glow. French inventor Georges Claude experimented with mixing the neon with other gases to make different colors. He displayed the first neon sign at the 1910 Paris Expo.

Guess what?

A Packard car dealership in Los Angeles was the first U.S. company to display neon signs.

Nn

Outboard Motor

Cameron Waterman invented the outboard motor in 1905. He started with a motorcycle engine and added a propeller and a tiller to it.

Guess what?

Ole Evinrude is often given credit for inventing the outboard motor even though he wasn't the first to build one.

Guess what?

At first, potato chips were called Saratoga Chips.

Potato Chip

The potato chip was invented in 1853 by George Crum, a chef in Saratoga Springs, New York. A customer complained that the French fries were too thick and soggy. So Crum cut a potato into thin slices and fried them until they were crisp.

Qq

Quartz Clock

Warren Marrison was an engineer who worked for Bell Laboratories in Canada. In 1927, he discovered that quartz crystals could be used to make clocks keep time more accurately. Quartz is a common mineral found in the earth's crust.

Guess what?

In 1969, Seiko became the first watch company to use quartz crystals in wristwatches.

Roller Skates

The first person known to have worn roller skates was Joseph Merlin, who wore them to a party in 1760. In 1819, M. Petitbled of France became the first inventor to patent roller skates. These early skates were in-line skates with metal or wooden wheels.

Guess what.?

Roller skates with four wheels were invented by James Plimpton in 1863.

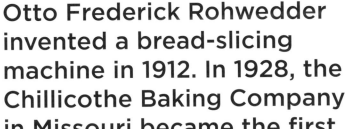

Sliced Bread

Otto Frederick Rohwedder invented a bread-slicing machine in 1912. In 1928, the Chillicothe Baking Company in Missouri became the first bakery to sell loaves of sliced bread.

Guess what?

A factory fire in 1917 destroyed Otto Rohwedder's first bread slicer and he had to recreate it.

Ss

Trampoline

The trampoline was invented by George Nissen in the 1930s. He got the idea from watching trapeze artists in the circus bounce in their safety nets when they landed. Nissen was a gymnast. He performed tumbling acts on the trampoline all over the world.

Guess what?

George Nissen named his invention after the Spanish word for diving board, *trampolín*.

Tt

Uu

Guess what?

In ancient times, only rulers and other very rich people had umbrellas.

Umbrella

The umbrella has been around for thousands of years. The first umbrellas were used to shade people from the sun. Later, people made them waterproof.

Vacuum Cleaner

Ives McGaffey invented the vacuum cleaner in 1868. It was called the Whirlwind and worked with a hand crank. Various kinds of vacuum cleaners with engines or motors were invented in the early 1900s.

Guess what?

The Puffing Billy was a huge vacuum cleaner that was pulled in a wagon. Long hoses were attached to it and brought inside to clean the rugs.

Vv

Windshield Wiper

Mary Anderson invented windshield wipers in 1903. The driver operated them with a lever inside the car. By 1916, most cars had windshield wipers.

Guess what?

Mary Anderson got her idea while riding streetcars. She noticed that the drivers had to either keep the windows open or stop to wipe off the windshield.

Ww

SCHOOL BUS

Guess what.?

The marimba, a South American instrument, was adapted from the xylophone.

Xylophone

The xylophone is a musical instrument from Asia and Africa. It was invented thousands of years ago. It has a row of different-sized bars that make different notes when hit with a mallet.

Yy

Yo-Yo

Guess what?

The yo-yo is thought to be the second-oldest toy in the world, after the doll.

The yo-yo was invented by the ancient Greeks and spread to Europe and Asia. But it wasn't commonly called a yo-yo until the late 1920s, when Filipino Pedro Flores started the Yo-Yo Manufacturing Company in California.

Zeppelin

Guess what?

Zeppelins were also used for travel until the crash of the Hindenburg in 1937.

A zeppelin is a type of rigid airship patented in 1895 by German Count Ferdinand von Zeppelin. Germany used zeppelins as warships in World War I, but they were not very good for that because they were easy to shoot down.

Zz

Glossary

accurate – free of errors.

bellow – a device with a flexible pouch that can be squeezed to blow air into something.

bladder – the organ in the body that stores urine.

bounce – to spring up after hitting a surface.

crank – a handle that is attached to a shaft and turned to start or run a device.

credit – recognition or honor.

dealership – a place authorized to sell specific products in a limited area.

design – 1) to plan how something will appear or work. 2) a decorative pattern.

hydrogen – a chemical element that is a colorless, odorless gas.

latex – a mixture of water and tiny bits of man-made rubber or plastic.

lawyer – a person whose job it is to know the law and to speak for people in court.

lever – a handle used to control or operate a device.

mallet – a light hammer with a padded head used for playing some instruments.

mineral – a naturally occurring, solid substance that is not animal or vegetable, such as gold, ore, and stone.

neon – a chemical element that is a colorless, odorless gas.

patent – an official document giving one person the right to make, use, or sell an invention.

perform – to do something in front of an audience.

propeller – a device with blades used to move a vehicle such as an airplane or a boat.

quartz – a hard, common mineral that can be clear or brightly colored.

reel – a device that turns or spins.

resin – a sticky substance that flows from some trees.

rigid – not flexible.

silo – a round tower used to store corn and other grains.

slicer – a tool that can cut something into thin pieces.

tiller – a lever used to steer a boat.

trapeze – a high, swinging bar that acrobats perform tricks on, usually at a circus.

wristwatch – a small clock on a strap that is fastened around the wrist.

More Inventions!

Can you learn about these inventions too?

airplane	helicopter	penicillin
automobile	hole punch	perfume
ballpoint pen	ice cream	radio
bicycle	ice cube tray	razor
blue jeans	iron	robot
camera	jet engine	safety pin
cell phone	jukebox	scissors
computer	Kevlar	skateboard
dishwasher	keyboard	steamboat
dynamite	lie detector	telescope
elastic	lightbulb	toilet
elevator	microscope	toothpaste
flashlight	mirror	vending machine
football	motorcycle	video tape
gas mask	nail polish	water fountain
glass	necktie	wheelchair
glue	odometer	X-ray
guitar	parachute	zipper